Thank you for teaching me to...

You make me strive to be a better...

The funniest thing you ever did was...

You are really great at...

I love that you are so passionate about...

My favorite thing about you is...

I have unforgettable memories of the time we...

I am grateful you are my coach because...

You make practice fun because...

I'll always remember when we...

Three words to describe you are...

You truly inspire me to...

The best day we had this season was...

You are special to me because...